The Kids' Joke Book

The Kids' Joke Book

Hundreds of barmy, batty, brainless

jokes that you will love to bits !

Collected and Illustrated

by Peter Coupe

INDEX

Published by Arcturus Publishing Limited
For Index
Unit 1
Henson Way
Kettering
Northants
NN16 8PX

This edition published 2000

Text layout and design by
Zeta @ Moo Design
Illustrations by Peter Coupe
Edited by Anne Fennell

Printed and bound in China

ISBN 1 84193 034 2

CONTENTS

AWESOME ALIENS

What do you give a sick alien ?

Planetcetamol !

What lights do aliens switch on every Saturday ?

Satellites !

What game do aliens play to while away the hours in deep space ?

Moonopoly !

Where do alien children go in the evenings ?

Rocket and Roll concerts !

What are wealthy aliens members of ?

The Jet Set !

Where do aliens go to study their GCSEs ?

High School (Very High School) !

Why do aliens never starve in space ?

Because they always know where to find a Mars, a Galaxy and a Milky Way !

What do evil aliens eat for lunch ?

Beans on toast - (Human Beans on toast) !!

Why are aliens good for the environment ?

Because they are green !

What do aliens have to do before they can drive a rocket at twice the speed of light in deep space ?

Reverse it out of the garage !

What do aliens call junk food ?

Unidentified Frying Objects !

How do you know when aliens are envious ?

Easy - they turn green !

What sort of sweets do Martian cannibals eat ?

Martian mallows !

Where do aliens go to study rocket science ?

Mooniversity !

How do you know when an alien is homesick ?

He just moons about all over the place !

Where do aliens live ?

In green houses !

★

What do you call a sad spaceship ?

An unidentified crying object !

★

How do you contact someone who lives on
Saturn ?

Give them a ring !

★

How do you communicate with aliens out in deep space ?

You have to shout really loudly !

★

What do you call an alien girl band ?

The Space Girls !

What do you call a mad alien ?

A Lunatic !

What game do nasty aliens play with Earth spaceships ?

Shuttlecocks !

What is the name of the planet inhabited by video recorders ?

Planet of the Tapes !

What ticket do you ask for to go there for a holiday ?

Return to the Planet of the Tapes !

Which side of a spaceship passes closest to the planets ?

The Outside !

Why did the impressionist crash through the ceiling ?

He was taking off a rocket taking off !

What does an alien gardener do with his hedges ?

Eclipse them every Spring !

★

Why did the alien buy a pocket computer ?

So he could work out how many pockets he has !

How can you tell if a computer is a show off ?

It will have a chip on its shoulder !

How do you get directions in deep space ?

Askeroid !

Where do aliens keep fish they capture from other planets ?

In a planetarium !

Why did the alien school have no computers ?

Because someone ate all the apples !

What do evil aliens grind up to make a hot drink?

Coffee beings!

What do you call an alien who travels through space on a ketchup bottle?

A flying saucer!

★

Why did the attendant turn spaceships away from the lunar car park?

It was a full moon!

How does a Martian know he's attractive ?

When bits of metal stick to him !

What do you call a spaceship made from cow pats ?

A Pooh F O !

Where do alien spaceship pilots go to learn how to fly in the darkness of outer space ?

Night school !

What do giant space monsters play to relax ?

Squash !

What does the alien from planet X use to smooth her nails ?

The X Files, of course !

Why are alien gardeners so good ?

Because they have green fingers !

What do alien children do on Halloween ?

They go from door to door dressed as humans !

How do you know if there is an alien in your house ?

There will be a spaceship parked in the garden !

What is the quickest way to get an alien baby
to sleep ?

Rocket !

How do you tell if an alien is embarrased ?

It blushes - and its cheeks go purple !

How do you catch a Venusian mega mouse ?

In a Venusian mega mouse trap !

What do you give a sick alien ?

Paracetamoons !

Where do aliens do their shopping ?

In a greengrocers !

Why do some aliens make their spaceships out
of twisted planks of wood ?

So they can travel at warp speed !

Who is in love with the alien james Bond ?

Miss Mooneypenny !

Where do aliens go for holidays ?

Lanzarocket !

What do aliens put on their cakes ?

Mars - ipan !

Who is the aliens' favourite robot cartoon character ?

Tin - Tin !

Why was the robot rubbing its joints with a video ?

Because it was a video of Grease !

What is a robot's favourite chocolate ?

Whole Nut !

Where are parts for robots made ?

In Bolton, Knutsford and Leeds !

What do you give a robot who fancies a light snack ?

Some 60 watt bulbs !

What did the teacher give the alien monster for lunch ?

Class 4B !

What sort of music do robots like best ?

Steel band music !

Who do robots vote for in a General Election ?

Tinny Blair !

How do you know when a robot has been in your fridge ?

There are footprints in the butter !

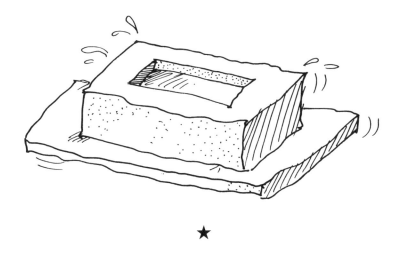

How do you invite a robot to a party ?

Send round a tinvitation !

★

What firework do aliens like best ?

Rockets !

What is an alien's favourite TV programme?

Blind date - it's the only way they can get a human girlfriend!

What do you call computer controlled sandpaper?

Science Friction!

What do aliens use to fuel their time machines?

Herbs!

If an alien leaves his chewing gum orbiting the Earth - what do you call it?

A Chew - F - O!

BATTY BRAIN TEASERS

How do you stop a head cold going to your chest ?

Easy – tie a knot in your neck !

Why shouldn't you try to swim on a full stomach?

Because it's easier to swim on a full swimming pool!

What creature sticks to the bottom of sheep ships?

Baaa - nacles!

How do you know if your little brother is turning into a 'fridge?

See if a little light comes on whenever he opens his mouth!

What is the coldest part of the North Pole?

An explorer's nose!

What do computer operators eat for lunch ?

Chips !

Why is that man standing in the sink ?

He's a tap dancer !

★

Where do rabbits learn to fly ?

In the Hare Force !

How did the witch know she was getting better ?

Because the doctor let her get out of bed for a spell !

What did the witch call her baby daughter ?

Wanda !

How do witch children listen to stories ?

Spellbound !

'Which witch went to Ipswich ?
The rich witch called little Mitch,
with the light switch for the soccer pitch,
who twitched and fell in a ditch;
that witch went to Ipswich –
and never came home !

What would you find in a rabbit's library ?

Bucks !

Why can you never swindle a snake ?

Because it's impossible to pull its leg !

What did the overweight ballet dancer perform ?

The dance of the sugar plump fairy !

Why is it easy to swindle a sheep ?

Because it is so easy to pull the wool over its eyes !

Why did the carpenter go to the doctor ?

He had a saw hand !

What do elves eat at parties ?

Fairy cakes !

What do you get if you cross a brain surgeon and a herd of cows ?

Cow-operation !

What is the only true cure for dandruff ?

Baldness !

What should you buy if your hair falls out ?

A good vacuum cleaner !

A man went to see his doctor with a brick
buried in his head.
What was he suffering from ?

Falling arches !

Why did the doctor operate on the man who
swallowed a pink biro ?

He had a cute-pen-inside-is !

Nurse - why are you putting Mr Smith's left leg
in plaster, it's his right
leg that's broken ?!

It's OK, I'm new so I'm practising on the left one
first to make sure I do it properly!

What sort of fish would you find in
a bird cage ?

A Perch !

★

What sort of fish would you find in a shoe ?

An Eel !

What sort of dance do fish do at parties ?

The Conga !

Where did the dog breeder keep his savings ?

In bark-lays bank !

Did you hear about the bungee jumper who
shot up and down for 3 hours
before they could bring him under control ?

He had a yo-yo in his pocket !

What do you call a cowboy who helps out in a
school ?

The Deputy Head !

What do you call the teacher in the school who gives out forms that you have to fill in ?

The Form Teacher !

★

Did you hear about the dog who was arrested ?

He didn't pay a barking ticket !

★

Where did the rich cat live ?

In a mews cottage !

★

What position did the witch play in the football team ?

Sweeper !

What position did the pile of wood play in the football team ?

De-fence !

Why couldn't the slow boxer get a drink at the party ?

Because everyone beat him to the punch !

Why was the archaeologist upset ?

His job was in ruins !

Why was the butcher worried ?

His job was at steak !

Why did the teacher have to turn the lights on ?

Because his pupils were so dim !

Why did the French farmer only keep the one chicken ?

Because in France one egg is un oeuff !

What did the farmer say when all his cows charged him at once ?

I'm on the horns of a dilemma here !

What sort of snake will tell on you ?

A grass snake !

Why did the doll blush ?

Because she saw the Teddy Bear !

POINTLESS INVENTIONS...

Camouflage for stick insects !

Disposable rubbish bags !

Colour radio !

Invisible traffic lights !

Plastic tea bags !

Waterproof soap !

Fireproof petrol !

What sort of ring is always square ?

A boxing ring !

What sort of queue is always straight ?

A snooker cue !

What sort of net is useless for catching fish ?

A football net !

Why do people leave letters at the football ground ?

They want to catch the last goal-post !

I've got a terrible fat belly !

Have you tried to diet ?

Yes, but whatever colour I use it still looks fat !

What do you call a frog that helps children safely across the street ?

The green cross toad !

Did you hear about the posh chef with an attitue problem ?

He had a french fried potato on his shoulder !

Why do golfers carry a spare sock?

Because they might get a hole in one!

★

A rather dim gardener from Leeds,
once swallowed a packet of seeds.
In just a few weeks,
his ears turned to leeks,
and his hair was a tangle of weeds!

★

I once met a man from Hong Kong,
who'd been jogging for twenty years long.
He was terribly sweaty,
- he looked like a yeti,
and his feet had a terrible pong!

What book do you buy to teach children how to fight ?

A scrapbook !

What sort of animals make the best TV presenters ?

Gnus - readers !

What sort of animal is best at getting up in the morning ?

A LLama clock !

I hear you've just invented gunpowder ?

Yes, I was using some candles to light my laboratory and it came to me in a flash !

How is your other invention coming along - you know, the matches ?

Oh ! They've been a striking success !

Why did the doctor take his nose to pieces ?

He wanted to see what made it run !

Why is it dangerous to tell jokes to Humpty Dumpty ?

He might crack up !

Blenkinsop - stop acting the fool - I'm in charge of this class, not you !

Why do pens get sent to prison ?

To do long sentences !

What was the parrot doing in prison ?

It was a jail-bird !

What is the name of the detective who sings
quietly to himself while
solving crimes ?

Sherlock Hums !

Why did the farmer feed his pigs sugar and
vinegar ?

He wanted sweet and sour pork !

Did you hear about the Scottish dentist ?

Phil McCavity !

Why is the soil in my garden always dry ?

Because you have leeks !

What kind of rose has bark ?

A dog rose !

What did the little boy say when he wanted his big brother to give him back his building bricks ?

Lego !

CRAZY CROSSES

What do you get if you cross a flock of sheep
and a radiator ?

Central bleating !

What do you get if you cross a pig with a
naked person ?

Streaky bacon !

What do you get if you cross a box of matches
and a giant ?

The big match !

What do you get if you cross a kangaroo with
a skyscraper ?

A high jumper !

What do you get if you cross a road with a
safari park ?

Double yellow lions !

What do you get if you cross an artist with a
policeman ?

A brush with the law !

What do you get if you cross an overweight
golfer and a pair of very tight
trousers ?

A hole in one !

What do you get if you cross a plumber with a
field of cow pats ?

The poohed piper !

How would you describe the behaviour of an elephant crossed with a bottle of whisky?

Trunk and disorderly!

What do you get if you cross a sheep and a spaceship?

Apollo neck woolly jumpers!

★

What do you get if you cross a skunk and a pair of tennis rackets?

Ping pong!

What do you get if you cross a pudding and a cow pat ?

A smelly jelly !

What do you get if you cross a pig and a box of itching powder ?

Pork scratching !

What do you get if you cross a bear with a freezer ?

A teddy brrrrrr !

What do you get if you cross a computer with a vampire ?

Something new fangled !

What do you get if you cross a tin opener, a vampire and a cricket team?

An opening bat!

What do you get if you cross a cow with a grass cutter?

A lawn mooer!

What do you get if you cross an ice cream with a dog?

Frost-bite!

What do you get if you cross a helicopter with a cornish pasty ?

Something pie in the sky !

What do you get if you cross a pair of dogs with a hairdresser ?

A shampoodle and setter !

What do you get if you cross a shoulder bag with a Mallard ?

A ducksack !

What do you get if you cross a dinosaur with a puppy ?

Tyrannosaurus Rex !

What do you get if you cross a football team
with a bunch of crazy jokers ?

Mad jester united !

What do you get if you cross a Viking and a
detective ?

Inspector Norse!

What do you get if you cross a large computer
and a beefburger ?

A big Mac !

What do you get if you cross an overheating large computer with a beefburger?

A big Mac and fries !

What do you get if you cross a hat factory and a field of cows ?

A pat on the head !

What do you get if you cross a mouse and a bottle of olive oil ?

A squeak that oils itself !

What do you get if you cross a jogger with an apple pie ?

Puff pastry !

What do you get if you cross a detective with a cat ?

A peeping Tom !

What do you get if you cross a TV programme and a load of sheep ?

A flock-U-mentary !

What do you get if you cross a footballer and a mythical creature ?

A centaur forward !

What do you get if you cross an actress and a glove puppet ?

Sooty and Streep !

What do you get if you cross a pasty and a scary film ?

A Cornish nasty !

What do you get if you cross a pig and a part in a film ?

A ham roll !

What do you get if you cross a sports reporter with a vegetable ?

A common tater !

What do you get if you cross a wireless with a hairdresser ?

Radio waves !

★

What do you get if you cross a hairdresser and a bucket of cement ?

Permanent waves !

★

What do you get if you cross a toadstool and a full suitcase ?

Not mushroom to put your holiday clothes !

What do you get if you cross a dog with a vampire ?

A were - woof !

What do you get if you cross an alligator and King Midas ?

A croc of gold !

What do you get if you cross a bike and a rose ?

Bicycle petals !

What do you get if you cross a tortoise and a storm ?

An 'I'm not in a hurry cane !'

What do you get if you cross a chicken with a pod ?

Chick peas !

What do you get if you cross a computer with a potato ?

Micro chips !

What do you get if you cross a dog with a maze ?

A labyrinth !

What do you get if you cross a plank of wood and a pencil ?

A drawing board !

What do you get if you cross a crocodile with a camera ?

A snapshot !

What do you get if you cross a chicken and an electricity socket ?

A battery hen !

What do you get if you cross a cow with a crystal ball ?

A message from the udder side !

What do you get if you cross a dog with a football ?

Spot - The - Ball !

What do you get if you cross a spider with a computer ?

A web page !

What do you get if you cross a toilet with a pop singer ?

Loo - Loo !

What do you get if you cross a frog with a traffic warden ?

Toad away !

What do you get if you cross a flea with some moon rock ?

A lunar - tick !

What do you get if you cross a vampire and a circus entertainer ?

Something that goes straight for the juggler vein !

What do you get if you cross a snake with a building site ?

A boa-constructor !

What do you get if you cross a parrot with an
alarm clock ?

Politics !

What do you get if you cross a bottle of
washing up liquid and a mouse ?

Bubble and squeak !

What do you get if you cross a mountain and a
baby ?

A cry for Alp !

What do you get if you cross a bunch of
flowers with some insects ?

Ants in your plants !

GHOSTLY GIGGLES

Which window cleaners do vampires use?

The one in pane - sylvania!

Why do monsters like to stand in a ring ?

They love being part of a vicious circle !

What do you call a ghostly teddy bear ?

Winnie the OOOoooooOoooohhHHhhhh !

Why do window cleaners hate vampires ?

They are a pane in the neck !

What do you call a Welsh ghost ?

Dai !

What do you call a tough Welsh ghost that
stars in an action movie ?

Dai Hard !

Why did the England cricket team consult a vampire ?

They wanted to put some bite into the opening bats !

Why did the vampire go to the blood donor centre ?

To get lunch !

How do vampires start a duel ?

They stand Drac to Drac !

★

When do ghosts wear red jackets and ride horses ?

When they go out fox haunting !

★

Why are owls so brave at night ?

Because they don't give a hoot for ghosts, monsters or vampires !

★

What did the old vampire say when he broke his teeth ?

Fangs for the memory !

★

Why do vampires holiday at the seaside ?

They love to be near the ghostguard stations !

What is the ghostly Prime Minister called ?

Tony Scare !

What do you call a dentist who really likes vampires ?

An extractor fan !

What do you call a futuristic android who comes back in time to plant seeds?

Germinator !

And what do you call his twin brother ?

Germinator II !

What do you call the ghost of the handkerchief ?

The Bogie man !

What sort of wolf can you wear ?

A wear wolf !

What sort of wolf delivers Christmas presents ?

Santa Claws !

What do you call a lazy skeleton ?

Bone Idle !

What do you call a ghostly would-be-Scottish King ?

Boney-Prince-Charlie !

Why do ghosts catch cold so easily ?

They get chilled to the marrow !

What do you call a scary, boney creature that staggers around making strange wailing noises ?

A supermodel making a record !

Why are skeletons no good at telling lies ?

Because you can see right through them !

What should you say when a vampire gives you a present ?

Fang you very much !

Why do vampires hate modern things ?

Because they hate anything new fangled !

Why did the ghost get the job he applied for ?

He was clearly the best candidate !

What do you call a ghostly haircut with long curly strands of hair ?

Deadlocks !

What do ghosts and vampires use to clean their pots and pans ?

Scarey liquid !

What do ghosts like with their food ?

A little whine !

What film is about a scarey train robber ?

Ghost Buster !

Where do ghosts live ?

In flats !

Where do vampires like to go for their holidays ?

The Dead Sea !

Why did the two vampire bats get married ?

Because they were heels over heads in love !

What did the pirate get when he smashed a
skeleton up in a fight ?

A skull and very cross bones !

Where do skeletons cook their meals ?

In a skullery !

What do you call a young skeleton in a cap and uniform ?

A skullboy !

Why did the skeleton fall into a hole ?

It was a grave mistake !

What villain does the spooky 007 fight ?

Ghoulfinger !

Why are hyenas always falling out ?

They always have a bone to pick with each other !

Who delivers Christmas presents to vampires ?

Sack-ula !

What vampire can you wear to protect you from the rain ?

Mac - ula !

What is the fairytale about a girl who falls in love with a really ugly loaf of bread ?

Beauty and the yeast !

When they got married, what sort of children
did they have ?

Bun-shees !

Why did Goldilocks go to Egypt ?

She wanted to see the mummy bear !

And, speaking of Mummies...

Mummy, mummy, what is a vampire ?

Be quiet and eat your soup before it clots !

Mummy, mummy, what is a werewolf?

Be quiet and comb your face!

Mummy, mummy I don't like my uncle Fred!

Well, just leave him on the side of your plate and eat the chips!

Mummy, mummy I don't want to go to America!

Be quiet and keep swimming!

★

Mummy, mummy I'm just going out for a quick bite to eat !

OK, but make sure you're back in your coffin before daybreak !

What did the monster say when the vampire asked for his daughter's hand in marriage ?

OK, we'll eat the rest !

Why do some ghosts paint themselves with black and white stripes ?

So they can frighten people on Pelican crossings !

OR

So they can play for Boocastle United !

What should you wear when you go out for a drink with a vampire ?

A metal collar !

What do you call a young woman who hunts vampires ?

A Miss Stake !

What do the police call it when they watch a vampire's house ?

A stake out !

★

What does the monster Tarzan eat for tea ?

Snake and pygmy pie with chips !

What did the ghostly show jumper always score ?

A clear round !

What did the young ghost call his mum and dad ?

His trans-parents !

Why don't you have to worry what you say to the werewolf computer engineer?

His bark is worse than his byte !

What sort of jokes do werewolves like best ?

Howlers !

What does a werewolf do when he meets a vampire?

He doesn't turn a hair!

Why wasn't the werewolf allowed to get off the lunar spaceship?

Because the moon was full!

★

Why did the werewolf start going to the gym?

Because he liked the changing rooms!

What did the train driver say to the werewolf?

Keep the change!

Why did the werewolf steal underwear when
the moon was full?

**Because his doctor told him a change was as
good as a vest!**

What sort of news do werewolves fear?

Silver bulletins!

Why did the shy werewolf hide in a cupboard
every full moon?

**Because he didn't like anyone to see him
changing!**

What form of self-defence do werewolves use ?

Coyote !

How do mummies knock on doors ?

They wrap as hard as they can !

Why was the *mummy* done up in brightly
coloured sparkly paper ?

He was gift-wrapped !

What does it say on the *mummy's* garage
entrance ?

Toot, and come in !

KNOCK, KNOCK...

Knock, knock...
Who's there ?
Yula...
Yula Who ?
Yula pologise for not letting me in straight
away when you see who it is !

★

Knock, knock...
Who's there ?
CD's...
CD's Who ?
CD's fingers ? They're freezing - let me in !!

★

Knock, knock...
Who's there ?
Wyatt...
Wyatt Who ?
Wyatt you open the door and see ?!

★

Knock, knock...
Who's there ?
Ivan...
Ivan Who ?
Ivan idea you will know as soon as you open
the door !

Knock, knock...
Who's there ?
Toyah...
Toyah Who ?
Toyah have to ask the same question all the time ?!

Knock, knock...
Who's there ?
The Electricity Board also known as the
George...
**The Electricity Board also known as the
George Who ?**
The Electricity Board also known as the George
of the light brigade !?

Knock, knock...
Who's there ?
Wynn...
Wynn Who ?
Wynn de Cleaner !?

Knock, knock...
Who's there ?
Willy...
Willy Who ?
Willy lend me a street map, I'm a stranger in town !?

Knock, knock...
Who's there ?
Bea...
Bea Who ?
Bea good boy and let me in !

Knock, knock...
Who's there ?
Stan...
Stan Who ?
Stan in front of the window and you'll see who !

Knock, knock...
Who's there ?
The Steps...
WOW - you mean the hit band ?
No, just the steps up to your front door !

★

Knock, knock...
Who's there ?
Paula...
Paula Who ?
Paula door open a bit, my coat is trapped !

★

Knock, knock...
Who's there ?
Irma...
Irma Who ?
Irma little short of time - just open up !

Knock, knock...
Who's there ?
Ashley...
Bless you !

Knock, knock...
Who's there ?
Carrie...
Carrie Who ?
Carrie on like this and I'll have frozen to death
before I get in !

Knock, knock...
Who's there ?
Fred...
Fred Who ?
Fred you'll have to open the door to find out !

Knock, knock...
Who's there ?
Vidor...
Vidor Who ?
Vidor better open soon....!!

Knock, knock...
Who's there ?
Sara...
Sara Who ?

Sara man delivering milk here yesterday - do you
think he could deliver some to me too ? !

Knock, knock...
Who's there ?
Cole...
Cole Who ?
Cole out here - open up !

Knock, knock...
Who's there ?
Curley...
Curley Who ?
Curley self a good host - keeping your guests
waiting out here !

Knock, knock...
Who's there ?
Mandy...
Mandy Who ?
Mandy with tools, if you need any repair work
done ?!

Knock, knock...
Who's there ?
Freda...
Freda Who ?
Freda jolly good fellow...

Knock, knock...
Who's there ?
Piers...
Piers Who ?
Piers I've forgotten my key - open up, there's a good chap !

★

Knock, knock...
Who's there ?
Holly...
Holly Who ?
Holly up and open the door, I'm fleezing out here !

Knock, knock...
Who's there ?
Alpaca...
Alpaca Who ?
Alpaca suitcase and leave you if you don't give
me my own key !

Knock, knock...
Who's there ?
Major...
Major Who ?
Major ask that queston yet again didn't I ?!

Knock, knock...
Who's there ?
Joe...
Joe Who ?
Joe keep everybody waiting like this ?!

Knock, knock...
Who's there ?
Tia...
Tia Who ?
Tia mount of time I've wasted standing here....!?

Knock, knock...
Who's there ?
Norm...
Norm Who ?
Norm more Mr Nice Guy - OPEN THIS DOOR !

Knock, knock...
Who's there ?
Julian...
Julian Who ?
Julian on that door all day waiting for people
to knock ?

Knock, knock...
Who's there ?
Giraffe...
Giraffe Who ?
Giraffe to ask such stupid questions ?!

Knock, knock...
Who's there ?
Doctor...
Doctor Who ?
You've played this game before, haven't you !?

Knock, knock...
Who's there ?
Paul...
Paul Who ?
Paul the door open for me, I've got my hands full
of shopping bags !

★

Knock, knock...
Who's there ?
Postman Pat...
Have you got a parcel ?
No, but I've got a black and white cat !?

★

Knock, knock...
Who's there ?
Alison...
Alison Who ?
Alison at the keyhole sometimes...

★

Knock, knock...
Who's there ?
Isiah...
Isiah Who ?
Isiah than you - I'm up on the roof !

Knock, knock...

Who's there ?

London's...

London's who ?

Ah ! You cheated !   I'll bet you can hear the animals from there !

Knock, knock...

Who's there ?

Carib...

Carib Who ?

Was it the antlers that gave it away ?

Knock, knock...

Who's there ?

Jim...

Jim Who ?

Jim mind not asking the same old question over and over !

Knock, knock...
Who's there ?
Denise...
Denise Who ?
Denise are freezing in this short skirt !

Knock, knock...
Who's there ?
Carla...
Carla Who ?
Carla doctor - I feel terrible !

Knock, knock...
Who's there ?
Pop...
Pop Who ?
Pop down and unlock this door please !

POTTY POETRY

Mary had a little lamb,
and a little pony, too.
She put the pony in a field,
and the lamb into a stew!

Humpty Dumpty sat on a wall,
Humpty Dumpty had a great fall.
All the king's horses and
all the king's men,
thought it was really funny,
and asked him to do it again !

Simple Simon
met a pieman
going to the fair.
Said Simple Simon
to the pieman,
May I taste your wares ?
Said the pieman
to Simple Simon,
I don't sell wares
but you can try one of my pies if you like !

I wandered lonely as a cloud
that floats on high o'er hill and dell.
No-one would sit next to me
'cos I had made a nasty smell !

If you can pass exams,
while all about you are failing theirs,
you're a bigger swot than I am,
Gunga Din !

2b or not 2b
that is the question,
or should I just use a pen instead ?!

Little Miss Muffet
sat on her tuffet
eating her favourite lunch.
A giant went by
looking up to the sky
and Little Miss Muffet went 'CRUNCH'

★

Little Bo-Peep
has lost all her sheep,
which is why she's down at the job centre this
morning!

I went to the pictures tomorrow
I got a front row seat at the back
I bought a plain cake with some currants in
I ate it and gave it them back!

The animals went in two by two,
the elephant and the kangaroo,
the lion the tiger,
the cat and the dog,
the mouse the gorilla,
the rat and the frog,
but they could only find one dinosaur,
which is why they aren't around any more!

Little Jack Horner,
sat in the corner,
eating his apple pie,
he put in his thumb,
and pulled out a plum,
and said 'that's a funny looking apple !'

Hickory Dickory Dock,
6 mice ran up the clock.
The clock struck one,
but the other 5 got away with it !

Jack and Jill
went up the hill
to fetch a pail of water
Jack fell down
and broke his crown
and Jill said
I told you you shouldn't try and skateboard
down...

A green spotted alien from Mars
liked eating motorcycles and cars.
When people cried 'shame'
he said 'It's the same...
as you lot eating Mars bars !'

At lunchtime every schoolday,
Blenkinsop (the fat),
would eat his way through everything,
except the kitchen cat.
Two plates of chips, for starters,
a pack of crisps (or three),
then on to shepherds pie and beans,
washed down with mugs of tea.
Spaghetti Bolognese and rice,
it all went down a treat,
Chicken curry, very nice,
pasties (cheese and meat).
When all the savouries had been,
despatched into his belly,
he started on the sweet menu,
(say goodbye to the jelly !)
Rice pudding, jam and eccles cakes,
yogurt, custard, shortbread,
till suddenly he simply burst,
on the final slice of bread.

NUTTY NAMES

What do you call a man with a tree growing
out of his head?

Ed - Wood!

What do you call a woman with a sheep on her head ?

Baa - Baa - Ra !

★

What do you call a man who wears tissue paper trousers ?

Russell !

★

What do you call a nun with a washing machine on her head ?

Sister Matic !

★

Why did the man with a pony tail go to see his doctor ?

He was a little hoarse !

What do you call a witch flying through the skies ?

Broom Hilda !

How did the Prime Minister get to know the secret ?

Someone Blairted it out !

What did the idiot call his pet zebra ?

Spot !

What do you call a fish on the dining table ?

A Plaice mat !

What do you call a man made from toilet paper ?

Louie !

What do you call a very tidy woman ?

Anita House !

What do you call a vampire that can lift up cars ?

Jack -u - la !

What do you call a vampire in a raincoat ?

Mack - u - la !

What do you call a vampire Father Christmas ?

Sack - u - la !

What do you call a girl who lives on the same
street as a vampire ?

The girl necks door !

What do you call a man who forgets to put his
underpants on ?

Nicholas !

What do you call a horse that eats Indian food ?

Onion Bha - gee - gee !

What do you call the coldest mammal in the World ?

The Blue Whale !

What do you call a dog that makes a bolt for the door ?

Blacksmith !

What do you call a man who steals cows ?

A beef burgler !

What do you call a man with a pile of soil on his head ?

Doug !

What do you call a man after he has washed
the soil off his head ?

Dougless !

What do you call a girl with a railway ?

Victoria !

How does Posh Spice keep her husband under
control ?

He's at her Beckham call !

What do you call an overweight vicar who plays football ?

The roly - poly - holy - goalie !

What do you call a woman with sandpaper on her head ?

Sandie !

What do you call her sister who lives at the seaside ?

Sandie Shaw !

What do you call the largest computer you can buy ?

A Big Mac !

What do you call medicine for horses ?

Cough stirrup !

What do you call a pretend railway ?

A play station !

What do you call a man with a kilt over his head ?

Scott !

What do you call a man with a pig on his head ?

Hamlet !

What do you call a man with eggs on his head ?

Omelette !

What do you shout to the Frenchman at the back of the race ?

Camembert !

What do you call a woman with one leg shorter than the other ?

Eileen Dover !

What do you call a poster advertising the last teddy for sale ?

A one ted poster !

★

What do you call the dance that grown ups do
in the supermarket ?

The can-can !

★

What do you call a girl with a supermarket
checkout on her head ?

Tilly !

★

What do you call a mummy that washes up ?

Pharaoh liquid !

What do you call a Scottish racehorse rider ?

Jock - ey !

What do you call a pig with an itch ?

Pork scratching !

What do you call a rodent's carpet ?

A mouse mat !

How do you spell hungry horse using just 4 letters ?

M T G G !

What do you call a woman dressed up as a gang of motor repairers ?

Car - men !

What do you call a Welshman who writes lots of letters ?

Pen Gwyn !

What do you call a sweater that bounces ?

A Bungee Jumper !

What sort of food can you get in a pub run by
sheep ?

Baaa meals !

★

What do you call a female magician ?

Trixie !

★

What do you call well repaired holes in socks ?

Darned good !

★

What do you call a pop group made up of
animal doctors ?

Vet, vet, vet !

What do you call a postman with a cow on his head ?

Pat !

What do you call a woman who goes horse racing ?

Betty !

What do you call a woman who works in a bakers ?

Bunty !

What do you call a dinosaur that drinks PG Tips ?

A Tea Rex !

What do you call a man with a collection of fish photographs ?

The Prints of Whales !

(Yes, I know they're mammals really, but it was a good joke anyway !)

What do you call a man with this book on his head ?

Joe King !

What do you call a man with a football pitch on his head ?

Alf Time !

What do you call a man who cleans out toilets ?

Lou !

What do you call a man with the word LATER
painted on his head ?

Ron (Later Ron !)

What do you call a woman with a bicycle on her
head ?

Petal !

★

What do you call a woman with a computerised
piano on the side of her head ?

Cynthia !

What do you call a woman with a computerised paino on top of her head ?

Hyacinth !

Why did the man take his pet dogs to work with him ?

He was a Lab assistant !

What do you call a man with a load of sports equipment on his head ?

Jim !

What do you call a woman that people sit on ?

Cher !

What do you call a boy who is always making fun of people ?

Mickey !

★

What do you call a man with a load of flowers and vegetables growing on his head ?

Gordon !

★

What do you call a man with a spade on his head ?

Digby !

★

What do you call a woman with a boat on her head ?

Maude !

What do you call a Roman emperor with flu ?

Julius Sneezer !

What do you call a man with a sack full of stolen goods over his shoulder ?

Robin !

What do you call a girl with a star on her head ?

Stella !

What do you call a mad man with the moon on his head?

Lunar Dick!

What do you call a girl with a beach on her head?

Sandy!

What do you call her brother, the one with the seagulls on his head?

Cliff!

What do you call a secret store of food in a monastery?

Friar Tuck!

What do you call a DJ lying across a horse's back ?

Jimmy Saddle !

What do you call a man with a swarm round his head ?

A. B. Hive !

What do you call a woman with a short skirt on ?

Denise !

What do you call a man with debts ?

Bill !

What do you call a woman who throws her bills on the fire ?

Bernadette !

What do you call a man who is part man, part jungle cat ?

Richard the Lion Half !

Why did the girl have a horse on her head ?

Because she wanted a pony tail !

What do you call a man with a karaoke machine ?

Mike !

What do you call a man who checks the size of rabbit holes ?

A Burrow Surveyor !

What do you call a woman with a nut tree on her head ?

Hazel !

What do you call a failed lion tamer ?

Claude Bottom !

What do you call a woman with a cat on her head ?

Kitty !